Dedication

To my loving Husband

Neil Andrew Lloyd

Sunrise: 28 October 1970
Sunset: 8 August 2019

Love, always and forever, Elaine
X

Elaine Lloyd

I Believe in Angels

AUSTIN MACAULEY PUBLISHERS™

LONDON · CAMBRIDGE · NEW YORK · SHARJAH

All of the events in this memoir are true to the best of the author's memory. The views expressed in this memoir are solely those of the author.

A CIP catalogue record for this title is available from the British Library.

ISBN 9781398463967 (Paperback)
ISBN 9781398463974 (ePub e-book)

www.austinmacauley.com

First Published 2021
Austin Macauley Publishers Ltd®
1 Canada Square
Canary Wharf
London
E14 5AA

Acknowledgements

I would like to thank everyone, both in this life and the afterlife.

My thanks go to my daughter Holly Alexandra Lloyd for the beautiful photo taken for the front cover of this book.

My gratitude goes to Nathan from the Production Team at Austin Macauley for preparing my second publication.

Table of Content

I Believe in Angels

Elaine Lloyd (nee Hadfield) was born on 5 June 1972, in East Manchester to loving parents. She first met Neil Lloyd in 1982 at Conway, in North Wales, and she told her mother then, that she would marry him one day... and she did!

Elaine had a normal upbringing and her ambition, in her teenage years, was to be an opera singer and "make it" in New York but, although she earned a Grade Eight at the Manchester School of Music, she was unsuccessful in hitting the bright lights of "The West End, in London, or Old Broadway," but she went down well enough at the Tameside Operatic and Dramatic Society and featuredin their popular shows until 1990.

Elaine, then worked in a Dog Parlour but, soon discovered she was allergic to dog fur, so she moved into office work where she met"the love of her life", Neil Lloyd, for the second time, in 1999.Neil, later proposed to her on the top of the Eiffel Tower, in Paris, and they were married in June 2004, in exotic Dominica. It was about this period that Elaine and Neil both discovered they had the gift of Mediumship, even though both of them had experienced many "spiritual events" during their younger days.

Elaine became a card-reader, while Neil developed and produced a variety of products to help people, who experienced connections with the "Spirit World". Nonetheless, while they were a very happycouple, who were blessed with two wonderful children, dark testing days were ahead for them all.

Chapter 1
My First Encounter

Where to begin? It must have been in mid-June of 1978, that I experienced my first encounter with the Spirit World. I was six years old and it was at this tender age that I first became aware that I am different from other girls and boys.

I remember it vividly, as though it were yesterday. It was at that tender age, one night, that I had a vision of myself flying over huge trees and bushes, then seeing my reflection in the river as I skimmed over it, although amazing, it was not the least bit frightening. I also viewed a most beautiful mansion below, with its pointed roof and remarkable grounds, that any girl could wish to see.

I will never forget telling my parents about my "dream", in the morning. Their reaction, not un-naturally, was one of shock, because they thought their youngest daughter had suddenly developed a wild, yet vivid, imagination. However, I realise now that it was not my imagination, it was reality! I had "Astral Travelled", to a place called Burton Hall which, later in life, I discovered still exists and is situated in Cheshire.

The feeling of love I experienced was overwhelming. I felt like a princess and didn't want my flying, over these wonderful grounds, to cease. Especially so, as two beautiful Angels had accompanied me during my flight. I knew I was safe, and felt protected, and so I wanted the experience to continue. As a little girl, I often spoke of my mansion experience and promised my parents that, when I was older, I would take them both for a visit to Burton Hall to see it for themselves.

Surprisingly, some forty years later, my amazing, beautiful mansion was offered as the prize in a competition! Naturally, I bought tickets to make my dream, to own the wonderful Hall, come true. But, sadly, I wasn't lucky in the draw. Nonetheless, I consoled myself that I had, at least, had the chance of entering the competition, because my experience, as a youngster, had made such a huge impression on me and my later life.

One thing is certain. Angels are real! They surround us all the time. I have seen them appear in paintings, photographs and even on my bedroom walls since I was a child and, they still visit me!

Chapter 2
My Second Encounter

The second encounter, with the Spirit world, was in 1978 on Christmas Eve.

I was giddy and excited, and could not wait for Santa to deliver my expected presents. I awoke in the early hours of the morning, to find a beautiful Angel with huge white wings and a white beard, standing at the foot of my bed. I recall closing my eyes tightly, then opening them again, just to make sure I wasn't dreaming! However, I soon fell asleep again, without opening my presents! When I did awake, I jumped out of my bed and, excitedly, told both my older sisters and my brother of my experience. They just smiled at me and gently admonished me by saying, "Elaine, stop romancing!"

But, I wasn't romancing! What I saw was real! One of my older siblings teased me and said it was Santa, who must have put on some "magic white wings"!

By doing much research, as I grew older, I discovered that the Angel, I had seen on that night, was a Warrior Angel. Also, after speaking to Mediums at Spiritualist churches they confirmed that what I had seen all those years ago was a Warrior Angel, and that they do exist. I was also told that, if you do see them, you are very blessed.

Chapter 3
Asthma Attack

In August 2008, while my husband was working away, I was admitted to hospital with a severe asthma attack. My son, who was then only two years old, bless him, rang for an ambulance, as my husband had left the telephone number in the front of our address book, in case there was ever an emergency in our household.

I was told by the Asthma Consultant that I had Allergy Asthma and, sadly, we would have to re-home our gorgeous Cocker Spaniel, Sky. However, there was also good news, in that later that evening, I was discharged and I went straight home to bed.

At that time, my Nana was one of my guides and I had the most beautiful visions of her looking so well and fresh faced. She put her hand upon my shoulder and said, "Elaine, you might find this very hard, but I want you to listen to me very carefully." This dream is so clear, that it was a though I had it only yesterday. I am so pleased that I am able to put this into writing, as it will give many people the confidence to know that we are all truly looked after, when our loved-ones go to the "other side of life."

This may come across as very strange, in that I was advised, by my Nana, to re-programme my brain, in effect, to tell my mind that I no longer had Asthma!

The next morning, I explained this to my family and they allthought I had gone mad! Most unfortunately, I also did as the Consultant told me and re-homed our lovely Cocker Spaniel. We were all heart-broken and the house felt so empty without our furry friend around the house. I kept taking the prescribed medicine and did as the Consultant had advised, but my heart and soul were telling me to take more notice of my dream.

This dream, I was told, was meant for a reason and, as I was so close to my Nana, I knew that she would never advise me to doanything that would make my health worse. However, I really was becoming worse by the day. I had re-homed the dog, which I still felt so bad about, and more importantly, it had no effect on my Asthma attacks, as I was, actually, becoming worse.

About a month later, Nana came to me again in a dream, this time she wasn't at all friendly. She was really angry, which was unlike my Nana. She shouted really loudly at me and said, "Elaine, please listen! This medicine is not agreeing with you. You need to stop taking it straight away!" Instead, I relied upon anti-histamine tablets.

The next few weeks went by and I decided, eventually, to listen to Spirit. So, I stopped taking all prescribed medicine and relied solely on an anti-asthma inhaler for emergencies only, but which I did notuse, as I gradually discovered that I no longer had Allergy Asthma.

So, here I am, ten years later and still Asthma free, with two splendid Airedale Terriers, who have just delivered a litter of eight lovely puppies comprised of five bonny boys and three gorgeous girls. It just goes to illustrate, in my opinion, that if you have a positive mindset, that miracles can, and sometimes do, happen. It certainly happened to me!

Always have faith in God and Spirit because they are here to guide us on our way, while we are here on Mother Earth.

God is within us all and we are all God's children. I have been so blessed in life, that I have been guided by Spirit and God, and Iearnestly pray that the person reading this book, will also have the same beautiful spiritual encounters that I have experienced. It really does open your eyes to the big, wide world we live in, that there is so much more to life than we currently know, or are even prepared to acknowledge.

Chapter 4
My Third Encounter

The Third Encounter happened, in March 2017, when I was involved in a serious car crash. I was on my way to a recruitment agency interview, so I could sign up to do some supply work inPrimary Schools.

I do try to wipe this experience out of my mind. It was raining heavily and I had, unfortunately, exited across a junction due to the slippery nature of the road surface, which caused the car to "aqua- plane" on the sodden tarmac. Initially, the impact knocked me unconscious and, as I came to, I became very frightened.

As my consciousness returned, I remember the Police, Ambulance and Fire Brigade sirens were still ringing out. It was quite an unholy cacophony! There I was, trapped in my crumpled car, and feeling panic stricken, because the paramedics were arguing with the firemen, who stated that my car could go up in flames at any time! It seemed somewhat insensitive to me, as I was still pinned in the wreckage!

Picture by courtesy of I.M.E. Law Claims Ltd.,
authorised and regulated by the
Solicitors' Regulation Authority.

Then I heard the sound of glass being smashed, so the paramedics could give me oxygen and, thankfully, the car roof was being sawn offso the firemen could extract me from the awful wreck. My whole body was bruised and burnt by the explosion of the ten air-bags that had done their job and prevented a worse outcome for me.

I prayed everything would turn out all right and that my legs were not badly injured. Due to the severity of the impact, my whole body had gone into shock.

Once the roof had been cut off, a caring fireman held my hand, and then covered my body with a silver sheet to keep me warm. He asked me several times, "can you feel your legs?" I replied, "No", but he continued to re-assure me that everything would be alright. He lay across me, on the silver sheet, to protect my body so that the glass,that had to be smashed, would fall on him and not on me.

Prior to my body being transferred to the spinal board, I was givena large dose of morphine. This is when my most amazing vision ever occurred! I saw my Nana with two beautiful Angels, one on either side of her, as they put me into the ambulance. I knew, at that point, I had been blessed once again, and that I would be alright.

After many scans, and checks by consultants, I was discharged from Manchester Royal Hospital, that same night! I walked out with all my family greeting me and telling me it was a miracle that I had survived. I was so happy, and I truly felt blessed, that I had been saved or protected by Angels and my Nana.

My two children were crying with joy and relief that I was alright and my husband made me laugh by calling me "a bloody nightmare", that had turned him into a nervous wreck.

The next morning my husband went to collect my CV documents from the car compound and I insisted that I should accompany him. My stomach turned when I saw my car crushed to half its normal size.

I noticed the white envelope on the passenger seat, with all my documents still in it.

No one, in the compound, could believe I had only suffered burnt lips and a few bruises on my body! The man, who was in charge of the compound said, "Someone was looking out for you yesterday." My reply was, "Well I do Believe in Angels!"

Chapter 5
My Fourth Encounter

This occurred in May 2017. My beautiful Dad had passed away the previous week in his armchair at home.

I had been to visit Dad, in the Ladysmith Building at Tameside Hospital, with my husband Neil and my son Owen, who was ten at the time.

My husband and son didn't enter the room, where my beautiful Dad was, they both sat in the bereavement waiting area, where you are allowed to put a message on the Remembrance Tree. Our son Owen put a heartfelt message on, which read, "Grandad, you will be in my heart forever."

Well, our private time with Dad was coming to an end, and I was called into the room for the last time. He looked so peaceful and seemed just to be asleep. I even smiled to myself thinking that any minute he would jump up and say, "Boo!" I held Dad's hand and told him that he was the best father that any daughter could wish for, and that I was proud that he was my Dad. I also told him that I would not be sad, as I had too many happy memories to remember.

As I was talking out aloud, and there was only my Dad and me in the room, I sensed a wonderful feeling come over me, and I knew that my Guardian Angels were with me. I felt the warm sensation all over my body, re-assuring me that everything was alright, and that my Dad was at peace.

It was so overwhelming, that I didn't want it to end. When I left the room, I explained, to the young lady at the Bereavement Centre, what I had experienced. She reassured me that it was nothing to be scared of, as Spirit, was simply there looking out for me.

Chapter 6
My Spiritual Awakening

In February 2018, my gorgeous loving husband, Neil, and I both experienced our Spiritual Awakening. I am glad that I didn't gothrough this on my own, but, sadly we were on the verge of splitting up, after being together for 20 years. We were no longer getting on and argued over the most silly, stupid little irritations. Examples are: who hadn't put the sauce back in the cupboard? Why wasn't his washing in the basket, but was left at the top of the stairs, for me to pick up, as usual? After all, I had been doing this for twenty years, why stop now?

It was at this low point in our lives, that Spirit intervened and gave me proof, so that all my dreams and seeing Spirits from a young age, began to make sense. Both Neil and I kept waking up at unusually early hours, especially between 3 and 5a.m., which I learned is the period when the veil, between our world and the Spirit World, is at its thinnest.

Under Spiritual guidance, I learned to meditate during these hours. Strangely, I also learned, during meditation, how water can heal everything in one's body, and how we are able to communicate with our minds, if we drink the good water.

Everything began to "click into place". My Nana came to me, in Spirit, and told me to bake bread. I had been baking it for the past few weeks, after finding a recipe on-line which, amazingly, turned out tobe my Nana's own recipe! That is when I believed, and knew, that we are all put on Mother Earth for a reason. It all made so much sense, that the reason I am here, is to give guidance and help to all awakeningsouls. I am now on *Linked-in* as a Spiritual Counsellor, Life Coach and Medium. I have helped very many people to come out of the dark and into the Light. I have also connected with some amazing Spiritual People, who have been through the same experiences as myself and I have also made some excellent, genuine, lovely caring and honest friendships.

I, absolutely, love the way the universe connects us all together.

Chapter 7
My Fifth Encounter

I really loved my fifth encounter with Spirit, as I went to bedabsolutely shattered, due to being up all night on the 18th February 2019, after our gorgeous Airedale, Roxy, gave birth to, at the time, six beautiful puppies. As I drifted off to sleep, my wonderful Dad came tome in a dream with a beautiful angel in the background. It was so clear. My father told me that Roxy would have eight, healthy puppies and one would be called Barney, which, oddly, was my Dad's nickname. It wasn't the first time I had had this dream, as I recall telling my eight-year-old daughter, Holly, the same dream weeks before the puppies were born.

Well, on Tuesday, 19th February 2019, I awoke at 6a.m. after only

having about two hours' sleep. I was so curious to see if any more puppies had been born, that I went downstairs. I was still half asleep, at the time, so I kept counting the puppies over and over again and, to my amazement, there were no longer six puppies, but eight!

There were three gorgeous girlsand five beautiful boys! I had ahuge smile on my face and I ran upstairs and woke my husband and the children. They justcouldn't believe it! Even Roxy's scan had shown only six puppies. I had also told the "Scan lady" that I thought there would be more and, further, that it would be nice to keep one and call it"Barney" after my Dad.

When the puppies were three weeks old, their new owners were allowed to view them. I had taken the precaution of asking for deposits over the 'phone, so that none of the new owners would be disappointed, lest the pups had already been spoken for.

One lady dropped out and I had a gentleman, called Paddy, on my list as "first reserve", as his son, Darren, had already reserved a puppy for himself. His father had recently had his dog, Ruby, put to sleep and had, previously, had an Airedale, Max. I rang up the gentleman and, to my surprise, he exhibited the same dry sense of humour as my Dad.

Well, when Paddy came to view the puppies, there were just two gorgeous boys remaining, Mr. Mint, the larger of the two, which really took to Paddy, so Mr. Orange was the puppy left for his son.

I was "over the moon" because two siblings would be together, and almost forgot to ask the gentleman what he was going to call the puppy, as we had simply given them names that related to the colourof their respective collars. The gentleman, Paddy, teasingly challenged me, "Well, aren't you going to ask me what name I have chosen for him?" I apologised and said I normally do, but that I had been overwhelmed that the two would be together! Paddy then said, "I'm calling this big fella, Barney." I had tears in my eyes and hemust have thought I was going crazy, when I told him that he had chosen my late father's name. Gallantly, he said, " I can change it to Dave if you like." I replied, " No, Barney, is the perfect name and suits him really well."

I have kept in touch with all of the new owners, and cannot wait to visit them in the near future, especially Barney. It goes to show that the universe listens to us all, and every day too!

Chapter 8
My Amazing Dream

A few days before my 47th birthday, my Nana and my Dad came to me in a dream, which was so real that, when I woke in the early hours, I actually believed it was real and in this dimension. My Nanatold me in a calm voice, to look after my Mum, and to tell her to be strong. In the background, was my Dad, smiling straight at me. The next words, from my Nana's mouth, were so heart melting, because 14 years before, I had lost a baby, whose gender I never knew. All I knew was that thelittle mite had a heartbeat andI was told that its loss was a blessing in disguise. The midwife explained to me that Iwould not have been able to carry the child

in my womb and, that if I had wished tocarry it to full term, there would have been much wrong with the poor, unfortunate little soul.

Well, for years now, every time I have visited a Spiritualist church, I always see a beautiful, gorgeous boy with blonde hair bouncing a great big blue ball. I have never known who he is. However, Nana confirmed to me that it was the little boy I had lost 14 years ago and, further, she told me he had never left my side, while I have been here on Mother Earth. My Dad was also there in the background but, he too, was very firm and endorsed it by saying, "You should haverealised that Spirit is connected to you."

Later, when I awoke, I shed tears of emotion, both happy and sad, because I had only just realised that this beautiful boy, that I keep seeing, was my first unborn child. Even though I found out 14 years later, it was such a joy to know that he is my child and such a beautiful little Angel.

I later had it confirmed, by another medium, that the boy was related to me but, because he was only in the early stages of his development, I had not realised this gorgeous child was related tome, as he would have been fourteen now. So why would my seeing aboy of about two, make me think it was my child that I lost so long ago? But, apparently, Spirit can show them at different ages, when they cross to the Spirit World. They can be seen, or come back, as a new-born, at their present age, or at other ages as they so choose.

I felt so blessed and touched by the dream, that I knew it to be true, as I have since had several encounters with Spirit getting in touch with me in this manner.

I think it is good news that, even though it was confirmed by a midwife/consultant that I would not be able to carry a child in my womb again, nonetheless, I was blessed once again by God and Inow always have a positive mind-set. So, twelve months later, I gave birth to a wonderful boy, who will turn 14 this year. He is a remarkable, polite young man, who is truly caring and makes me really proud he is my son. I am also blessed with a beautiful little girl, who will become ten this year. So, to all those people out there, who are being told they cannot have children, I say miracles can happen. If it has happened to me, then it can happen to you.

Chapter 9
My Sixth Encounter

This, my sixth encounter, occurred on the 24th of May 2019. I was unwinding by wallowing in our hot tub in the back garden. I lay there, meditating, for quite a while. By then, I felt very relaxed, "chilled out" as the Americans would say, but not in the sense of temperature. I was there, in the hot tub, for about two hours.

The sun was out and I was enjoying the sound of the lovely bird songs that bless our space. They were in full voice, then I looked up at the wonderful azure sky and suddenly caught sight of two beautiful Angels in the wispy clouds. My eight-year-old daughter was in the tub too, as she had just joined me for a warm relaxing soak, so I explained, to her what I had seen. I suggested she look for herself and, she too, saw them and described them to me. I then pointed out a wonderful "love heart" in the same area of sky.

It goes to show, in my view, that we are never alone and that we are surrounded, all the time, by marvellous Spirits. So, we should never have need to feel despondent, as we are all loved so very much. In fact, much more than we, still on Earth, yet realise.

Chapter 10
My Husband's Passing

On Tuesday, 6 August 2019, my beautiful husband came into my Angel Card Reading Session, while I was working for an on-lineorganisation which titles itself: *Psychic Sofa*.

Neil had a very trembling voice and shouted very loudly, "Elaine, I need you!" I came off the business line at once and found my dear husband vomiting blood into the sink. Straight away I rang for an ambulance, and it arrived in minutes. It was then that I realised how serious was my husband's condition.

Neil Andrew Lloyd was admitted to Hospital and was taken to the theatre straight away. Apparently, my husband had suffered a throat aneurysm. My wonderful Neil had three bands fitted internally and I was advised he would be home, fit and well, in a few days.

On the same Tuesday evening, I was informed my husband would need to have a blood transfusion, due to the blood loss he had sustained. However, the Hospital was sadly short staffed, so they gave Neil alternative (but unspecified) medication, that I was told would stop the blood loss.

On Wednesday morning, my family and I were then advised that more bands needed to be fitted but, unfortunately, they had to stop his internal bleeding, before they could put into effect this routine procedure, (which begs the question, "Why did they fit bands theprevious evening, if it was necessary to stop the bleeding prior to fitting the bands?).

Again, on Thursday morning, the bands were due to be fitted. I will never forget the telephone call I received direct from my dear husband that day. It was 8a.m. on 8 August, telling me not to bring thechildren, because he felt very weak and, further, said that the hospital had "messed up". He said he had heard the staff talking. He told me he loved me very much and he sounded so scared, bless him. Ireassured Neil, that there was nothing to worry about and said I would ring the hospital straight away. After speaking to a female member of the hospital staff, who I assumed was a nurse, I was given a confirmation that everything was "OK" with Neil and, she furthersaid, that she could not understand why he had said, "the hospital had messed up."

At 9a.m. I received another phone call, direct from the Hospital, asking me to go there immediately! I was there at 9-15a.m! I was toldthat my husband had suffered a cardiac arrest at 9-14a.m. and that the Hospital staff were very concerned about Neil's heart rate, which is why they made the urgent call for me to attend, "at once".

I begged to be allowed to go in to see Neil but, they said I could notas "a team of ten doctors/nurses were working on him". I dropped to my knees and pleaded because my husband was not breathing. So, eventually, they let me in.

It was the worst sight that I have ever seen! My heart sank! My beautiful husband had suffered his cardiac arrest a minute before I arrived. I knew, 100%, that they would bring him back, with me by his side. I yelled at the doctors, "Please! Please! Don't stop! Get the defibrillator out!" I held Neil's hand very tightly and felt a tightsqueeze back! The next minute, the nurse shouted out, "We've got a pulse!"

I felt so happy and thought I had saved Neil with my strong loving words and the healing energies that I was giving to Neil, but then three beautiful Angels appeared at the foot of his bed with his dear, loving father, standing next to them. I cried out, "Neil, please! No!" "You are not ready yet, to pass over to the Spirit World. Please come back to me and the children." In reply, Neil simply squeezed my hand eventighter.

My loving husband was then taken away and a doctor informed me that "they would stop the internal bleeding and my husband would be,

O.K." Neil was then put on a ventilator and I was so pleased, as he began breathing for himself and his heart rate was back to normal.

Nonetheless, and sometime later, a hand was then placed on my shoulder and a gentle voice said, "can I please have a word in private?" I agreed, and was taken to a small quiet Prayer Room, whereI was told that, "Unfortunately, your husband's internal bleeding couldn't be stopped, as we do not know where it is coming from. So, he will eventually bleed to death."

I became hysterical. I had my beautiful sister Debbie, niece Leah and a friend, Rod, at my side to help me through this terrible, heart- rending ordeal.

Unfortunately, my loving husband was given his Angel Wings far too young, at the age of 48. He passed over to the Spirit World, at 4pm, on the 8th of August 2019.

The lesson I took from this, was a life lesson; that we are all put on Mother Earth for a certain amount of time and when your life journey is over, it is over for you to explore your new adventure in the Spirit World, until you meet your loved ones again, and you will enjoy Eternal Life with them.

I was pleased that Neil's father came for him, and that Neil had his Guardian Angels by his side from the start to the finish during his hospital admission.

My gorgeous, loving husband, Neil, spent his first Christmas as an Angel in December 2019. God Bless him!

Neil has never left my side since he passed over, and is keeping me and the children strong.

Epilogue

Look to this day... For yesterday is but a dream
And tomorrow is only a vision
But, today, well lived
Makes every yesterday a dream of happiness
And every tomorrow a vision of hope.
Look well, therefore, to this day.

- A Sanskrit Proverb

Spiritual/Meditation Tools Created By My Late Husband

Spiritual Pyramids

Spiritual Pyramids

40

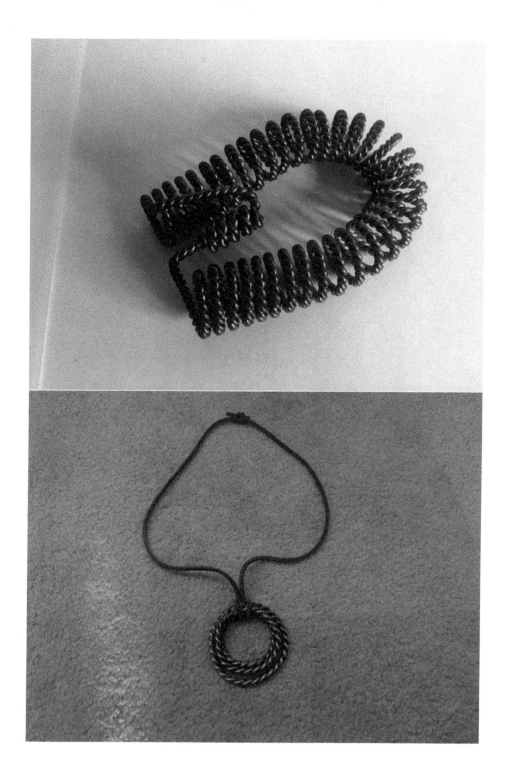

43

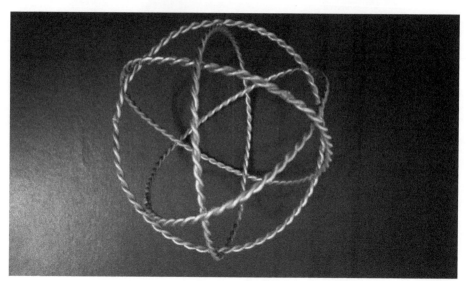

Copper Coils

Copper Healing Machine

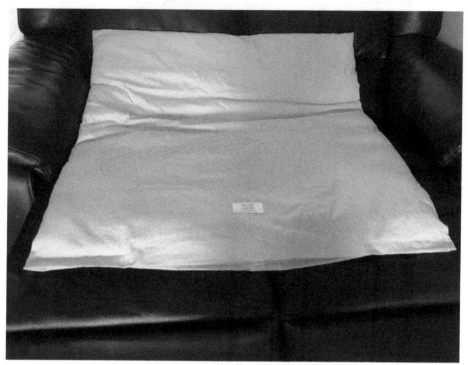

Healing Blanket Created and Blessed by Neil

Special Memories

Go Kart Kitted out in Dad's Memory - Black & White to symbolise Neil being a big Newcastle United Fan

Basketball now taken up too, Using No. 70 in memory of Dad

Dad's Creative Skills Shining Through His Gorgeous Princess - The Loomigurumi Queen

Elaine Lloyd Recording Her Song - I Believe in Angels - For Book Trial
as it Resonated With her Book - Dedicated to her Soul Mate

Carrying on her late husband's healing blanket/cushion business with a Christmas theme

Neil's Best Friends - They still look for him every day. Roxy & Riley the Airedale Teddy Bears

Neil in his Modelling Days

One of the best days of my life - Always be grateful for what you have and NEVER take anything for granted. Always take one day at a time

You are never alone

Neil & Owen in their go karting days

The Lanzarote/Hot Tub King

Sometimes you don't know what you had until it's gone

The Children gate crashing one of Dad's important business meetings -
It definitely broke the ice with his new business partner!

Sunset pic taken by Neil in Lanzarote

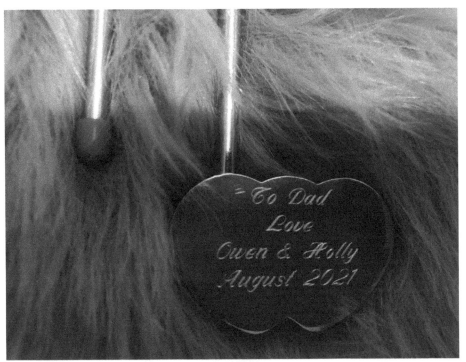

Love locks dedicated to Neil

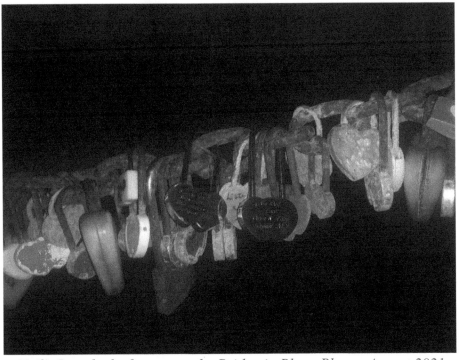

Neil's Love locks forever on the Bridge in Playa Blanca August 2021

Love Lock Bridge - Playa Blanca

Neil's Forever Bed

Where Neil turned his creative thoughts into reality. Playa Blanca, Lanzarote

Reflections on Neil's Life
with
A Tribute

from Elaine

My gorgeous Nee Nee, there is a very special place beyond the stars above, somewhere peaceful, yet full of light and love. Now you're in no pain, Nee Nee. Your soul is laid to rest. You're now safe with the angels, for they only take the best!

Always in our hearts 🖤 🖤

Reflection Music

I Will Always Love You
Whitney Houston

The Lord's Prayer

Our Father, who art in heaven,
hallowed be Thy name;
Thy Kingdom come;
Thy will be done,
on earth as it is in heaven.
Give us this day our daily bread.
And forgive us our trespasses,
as we forgive those who trespass against us.
And lead us not into temptation,
but deliver us from evil.
For Thine is the Kingdom,
the power and the glory,
for ever and ever.
Amen.

Final Blessing

Spiritual Quotes
and Sayings

United we are strong

divided we are weak

that's an advantage

others seek

- Nishka Tupacs

"When you
change the
way you look
at things,
the things you
look at
change."

-   Wayne Dyer

Life is like sailing.

You can use any wind

To go in any direction

- Robert Brault

**You are not wealthy until
you have something
money can't buy.**

-   Garth Brooks

Dream it.

Believe it.

Achieve it.

You create your reality

- Tony Robbins

YOUR WORDS CREATE

YOUR REALITY

- ROBERT TENNYSON STEVENS

**You'll never
find peace
of mind
until you
listen to
your heart.**

- George Michael

"Trust in the LORD with all your heart;

Do not depend on your own understanding.

Seek his will in all you do,

And he will show you which path to take."

- Proverbs 3:5-6 NLT

*Commit your
work to the Lord,
and then your
plans will succeed.*

-   Proverbs 16:3 NLT

You can do anything
if you put your mind to
it, the only thing that
can stop you is yourself

- Unknown

A bird sitting on a tree is never afraid of the branch breaking, because her trust is not in the branch but in her own wings. always believe in yourself.

- Charlie Wardle

You shall love the
Lord your God
with all your heart,
and with all your
soul, and with all
your mind, and
with all your strength.

- Mark 12:30

ANGEL
BLESSINGS

May you be showered with
Angel Blessings today! May
the angels bring you peace,
happiness, hope, and divine
comfort. May you be healed
of whatever causes you pain.
May your whole life be
filled with Divine Love and
Angelic Light!

- Unknown

Don't use your
energy to worry.
Use your energy
to believe.

- Joel Osteen

CONSTANTLY

Think about how you could be doing

THINGS BETTER

Keep questioning yourself.

- Elon Musk

Success Isn't
About How Much
Money You Make;
It's About The
Difference You
Make In People's
Lives.

-   Michelle Obama

GOD'S LOVE
CHANGES
EVERYTHING

-   Unknown

Pain makes you
stronger, tears make
you braver, and
heartbreaks make you
wiser, so thank the past
for a better future.

- Unknown

"Have the courage

to follow your

heart and intuition.

They somehow

know what you

truly want to become."

- Steve Jobs

Power without love is reckless and abusive, and lover without power is sentimental and anemic. Power at its best is love implementing the demands of justice, and justice at its best is power correcting everything that stands against love.

- Martin Luther King

Trust me, I

know what

I'm doing

-    The Universe

When you arise
in the morning,
think of what a
precious privilege it is

to be alive;

to breathe, to think,
to enjoy, to love.

- Marcus Aurelius

Everyone
Stumbles and
Falls. The issue
Is whether or
Not you get
Back up again.

- Proverbs 24:16

If you fall you
Get up and keep
Going from where
You are. You don't
Go back to the start.

- Unknown

It's

TOO LATE

To focus

On your

-    Anonymous

CPSIA information can be obtained
at www.ICGtesting.com
Printed in the USA
LVHW071916101121
702989LV00015B/557